This book is dedicated to our Earth
and to all living things that call it home.

Text copyright © Hollis Kurman 2023
Illustrations copyright © Barroux 2023
First published in Great Britain and the USA in 2023 by Otter-Barry Books,
Little Orchard, Burley Gate, Herefordshire, HR1 3QS
www.otterbarrybooks.com

ISBN 978-1-91307-416-6

Illustrated with watercolour

Set in Supernett Condensed

Printed in China

9 8 7 6 5 4 3 2 1

COUNTING iN GREEN

10 LITTLE WAYS TO HELP OUR BIG PLANET

Hollis Kurman ⊚ Illustrated by Barroux

Otter-Barry BOOKS

What can we do when Mother Earth needs our help?

From one to ten we're counting green to keep our planet safe and clean!

I New Tree

Let's plant a tree
to clean our air.

2 Breezy Wheels

Let's go by bike
to ride without polluting.

3 Meatless Meals

Let's eat less meat
to care for our planet, our animal friends
and ourselves.

4 Recycling Bins

Let's collect used things
to turn them into *new* things.

PAPER

GLASS

PLASTIC

5 Better Bags

Let's bring bags from home —
to say NO to plastic (it hurts the Earth).

6 Earth-Friendly Lights

Let's use long-life lightbulbs
to keep our lights shining.

7 Beach Pick-Ups

Let's clean up our beaches
to protect our seas and creatures.

8 Bathing Birds

Let's make birdbaths
to invite the birds to sip and splash.

9 Wild Flowers

Let's grow a garden
to welcome bees,
butterflies and bugs.

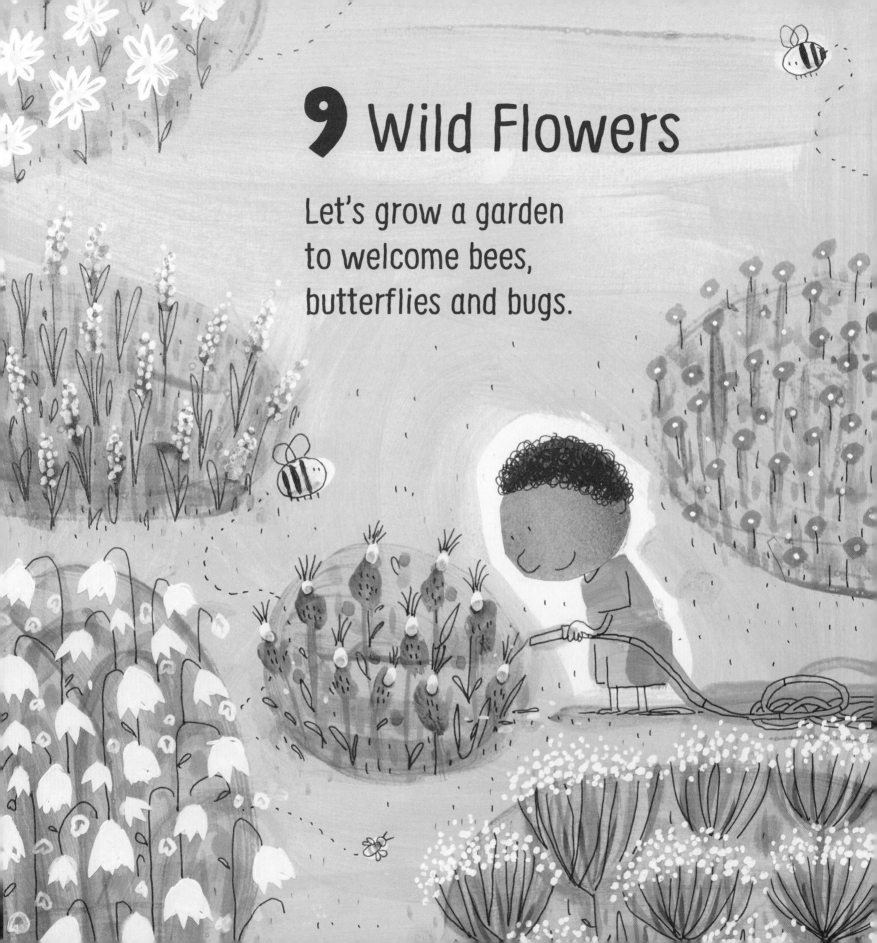

10 Friendly Neighbours

Let's all come together
to look after our green spaces.

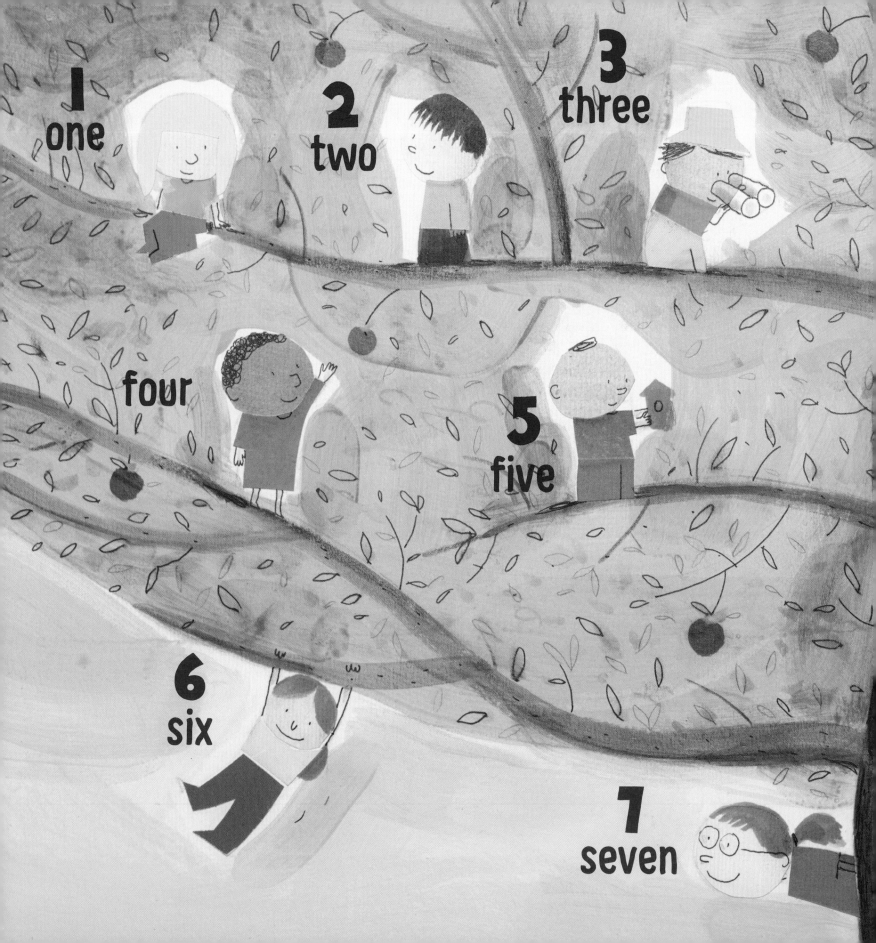

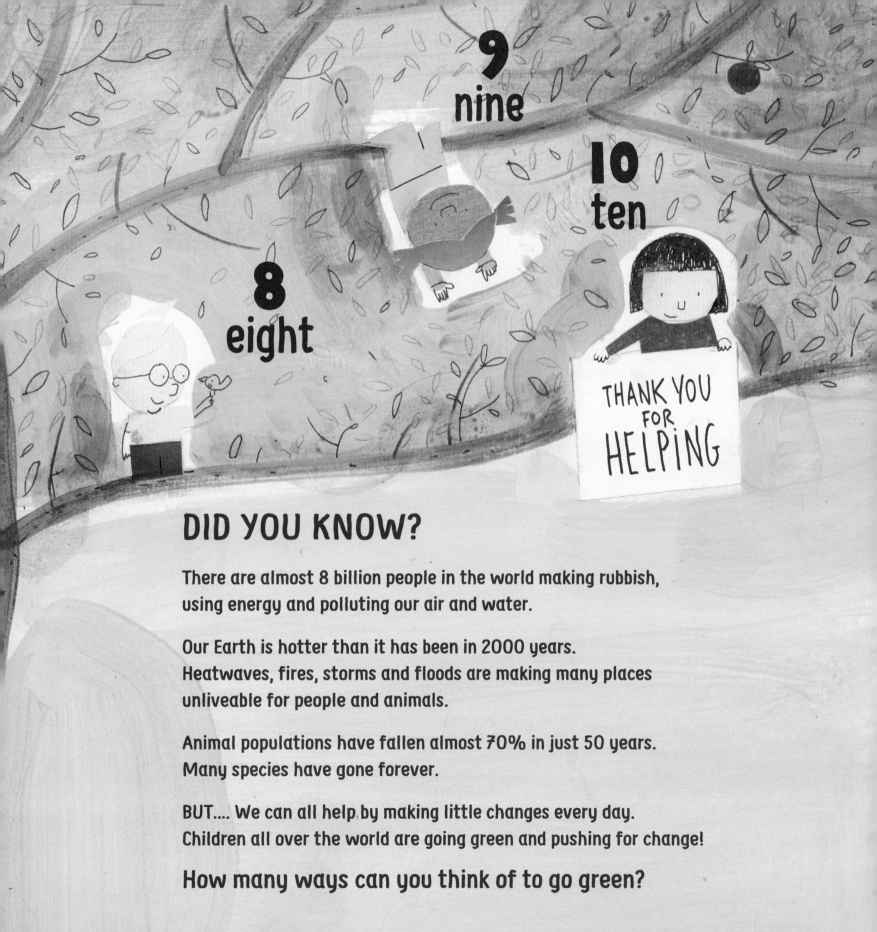

9 nine

10 ten

8 eight

THANK YOU FOR HELPING

DID YOU KNOW?

There are almost 8 billion people in the world making rubbish, using energy and polluting our air and water.

Our Earth is hotter than it has been in 2000 years.
Heatwaves, fires, storms and floods are making many places unliveable for people and animals.

Animal populations have fallen almost 70% in just 50 years.
Many species have gone forever.

BUT.... We can all help by making little changes every day.
Children all over the world are going green and pushing for change!

How many ways can you think of to go green?

OUR PLANET AND US

Everything on Earth is connected: people, plants, trees
and animals need each other to live.
Everything we do matters: what we eat, what we wear,
how we move and how we shop make a big difference.
Earth is our home. Let's keep it safe and clean.

DO YOU WANT TO HELP OR FIND OUT MORE?

**Here are some of the many organisations helping
the planet (and helping kids go green):**
World Wildlife Fund   www.worldwildlife.org
NASA Climate Kids   climatekids.nasa.gov
Greenpeace   www.greenpeace.org/international/explore/about
Young People's Trust for the Environment UK   ypte.org.uk
Friends of the Earth UK   friendsoftheearth.uk